MORE FEELINGS

by

Terry Funnell

More Feelings

Poems by
Terry Funnell

with
illustrations by
Peter Guest

The **Hallamshire** Press
1992

Published by The Hallamshire Press.
The Hallamshire Press is an imprint of
Interleaf Productions Limited
Exchange Works
Sidney Street
Sheffield S1 3QF
England

Typeset by Interleaf Productions Limited
and
Printed in Great Britain
by The Cromwell Press,
Wiltshire

British Library Cataloguing in Publication Data:

Funnell, Terry
More Feelings
I. Title
821.914

ISBN 1-874718-10-5

Contents

Preface

In this second book of verse (and a companion to the first volume, called simply *Feelings*), I have continued to look at life in all its many facets, and hope you may find something that will entertain, amuse or set you thinking. If you enjoyed *Feelings*, you will find the same mixture of the comic and the tragicomic, as well as a few thoughts on life, contained in these verses.

The inspiration for my poems has always come from observing the everyday dramas of those around me, and I've tried to capture in this collection some of the wonderful things people say and do. As we say in Yorkshire: "There's nowt so funny as folk", and so with that in mind, see if you can spot some of the folk you know. Or — heaven forbid — you might even see yourself!

Again, I'd like to thank my son-in-law, Peter Guest, for his excellent cartoons, my daughter Jill for typing up the poems in the first place, and the staff at Interleaf Productions for all their help.

Terry Funnell
November 1992

SINGLE

I've just had a friend round to stay for a while
And, oh dear, she has thrown my routine,
It's not that I minded her coming to stay:
Well I've treated her just like a queen.

It's just that on set days I do certain things
And I don't like my programme upset,
And what with her being about in the house
I did nothing but fuss round and fret.

Now take Mondays: I do all my washing,
I start right after breakfast at nine,
So by dinner time everything's through the machine
And I've got them all out on the line.

I'll p'raps have a doze after dinner
And I'll dust round my sideboard and shelf,
Then I get my tea ready, I'll p'raps just have toast,
And I've all evening then, to myself.

Tuesday mornings I've got to be early
'Cause I pay for my milk at the door,
He comes about seven, so I have to be up
Or he says he'll not call anymore.

Then I usually shop for my groceries
And that takes me best part of the day,
Then Tuesday's a good night on telly
So that passes my evening away.

I always vac round on a Wednesday:
It's surprising the dust I collect,
Then I go round the mantlepiece, sideboard and shelf
'Cause I like my house looking perfect.

I sometimes go out on a Thursday,
If it's nice I'll p'raps walk through the park,
But in winter I just lock my door and stay in:
Well I never go out after dark.

Friday morning is one of my best days,
My neighbour comes round for a chat,
And we always start laughing and joking —
Oh, I really enjoy doing that.

Friday evening I just watch the telly,
But it's boring for most of the time,
It seems to be sport on most channels
And I like a good mystery or crime.

On Saturday morning I bake things
Just in case someone calls by surprise,
I might do jam tarts or a custard,
If I've got apples in, I do pies.

After dinner I go to my neighbour's,
And most weekends I stop for my tea,
I stay quite a while, I know she doesn't mind,
'Cause we've nobody left her and me.

Now I really look forward to Sundays:
I go out to church about ten,
But I like to dust round just before I set off
So it's nice when I come home again.

I like "Sunday Half Hour" on the wireless,
Then I sit down and watch "Songs of Praise",
Then I get myself ready and go off to bed —
And that takes me through all seven days.

I suppose it's not very exciting,
But it's what I've done year after year,
And all being well, I'll keep doing the same,
That is of course, while I'm still here.

THE JOURNEY

When I was a boy I went slowly to school
And the time would meander apace,
The lessons were hard, and I wished that each hour
Would take to its heels in a race.

As a young man the days were for burning:
Not a minute would pass by unfilled,
In pursuit of a joy for the taking
Many precious achievements were spilled.

At twenty the world was for using:
Success was a goal to attain,
My friends were aplenty and laughter was cheap
When others were easy to blame.

When thirty came round I was moving,
There were still many shoes to be filled,
Confident I could take all the pressure on board:
What if some of the friendships were killed?

When I reached forty, things started changing,
For drive and ambition had waned,
Yet still there were laurels just out of my grasp
And prizes of worth to be gained.

Fifty years logged a steady achievement:
At the summit with nowhere to go,
Something lost, something won, something missing,
An account any balance would show.

Too young to retire at just sixty;
Too old for responsible work;
Too gifted to hand to another the tools
Of a craftsman to those of a clerk.

Now seventy years have passed by me,
Every one of them precious and rare,
Now the future holds fear and foreboding,
I see nothing but emptiness there.

I cannot complain or gain favour,
I have shared of life's pleasures in full,
But death is an unwelcome stranger
And I feel on my coat tails a pull.

Life is long as forever in boyhood;
Days are joyous adventures to fill,
Now the clock on the mantlepiece ticks off the hours
And soon my old timepiece will still.

Has it all been a journey to nowhere
On a train that will never arrive?
We never will know, for as each of us go
Not a single one lives to survive.

At best I will hope for a heaven;
At worst I will finish in hell,
But until that day I must ponder away,
For no one has come back to tell.

So now I die daily a little,
Not knowing the how, what or where,
My friends and relations make busy their days
While I am confined to this chair.

Alone I can smile at successes,
At my failures alone I can cry,
Alone and in limbo I now sit and wait
And alone, so alone, I will die.

UP THE POLL

I'm just off to the old polling station,
But who shall I vote for, and why?
You see, I think I'm one of them floaters
'Cause I don't know which party to try.

The local shopkeeper round our way
Said Conservatives would be the best,
And he seems a sensible fellow
So I'll vote them and discard the rest.

Then again, I heard all about Labour:
How they're spending more on NHS,
So I think I'll vote them, or else if I'm ill
I could be in a terrible mess.

Mind you, I think Liberals are super:
Paddy Ashdown has got good ideas,
So I think I'll vote Liberal and give them a chance
'Cause they've not been in power for years.

You see, I believe that we're all equal,
I suppose that's a Communist view,
And they say that Utopia's just round the bend
So I'll vote them and see how they do.

And yet the Green Party's a good one,
They'll look after rivers and fields,
So I think I'll vote them and turn a new leaf
By not eating red meat with my meals.

Then again, there's that Group Meditation,
They stand for the natural law,
And it might be quite jolly sat crossing my legs
And bouncing around on the floor.

There's the Monster Raving Loony lot,
I haven't considered them much,
I suppose if I go in and put my cross there
The Prime Minister would be Lord Sutch.

Well, here I am inside the station,
I'm not down on your list, do you say?
What, I've not paid my poll tax last April
So I can't have a vote anyway!

"You see, I think I'm one of them floaters
'Cause I don't know which party to try."

HYMN OF PRAISE

Lift to the skies your songs of joy,
Shout to the heavens above,
Praise the Creator's wondrous world,
Offer eternal love.

Give up on life's ambitious gain,
On humble pathways tread,
Turn from the banquet offered free,
Ask but for daily bread.

Open your hearts to pastures new,
Ever the learner be,
Listen and gain from all around,
Have done with bigotry.

Give to the world the best you have,
Treasure your honoured place,
You have but once to give your all,
Run while you're in the race.

Search for the lonely, help the poor,
Many have fallen by,
Hold out a hand to those in need,
Encourage all to try.

Journeying all we seek a goal,
Each to his own reward,
The word is out and the word is love,
And love is the word for Lord.

BOOKED

Good afternoon officer . . . . . . sergeant,
I must say, you've got a nice day,
And look at your helmet all shiny:
You've fair polished your cap badge away.

My goodness, you are a large fella,
You're a very big man for your size,
You must have been big even when you were small,
Did I mention you've got lovely eyes?

Are you stood by my car for a reason?
It's not that I'm bothered, of course,
But the wife's up the road with three carrier bags,
Have I told you? You just look like Morse.

Are these yellow lines here for a reason?
Only everywhere else was full up,
I've a flask of tea under the dashboard,
If you like I can give you a cup.

I'n't it funny how sometimes you miss things?
And this road is a little bit dark,
I think someone's been round here and painted these lines,
I swore they weren't here when I parked.

Have you been waiting long for me coming?
Only time simply flies when you're out,
It's good for you keeping an eye on it though
'Cause I've heard that there's car thieves about.

You'll laugh when you look at me tax disc,
I can see that there's no fooling you,
Only my neighbour said that just for a week
A brown Guinness label would do.

Then again, it's the same with me tyre,
It's worn down to the tread on that side,
Well I blame my wife for that, corporal,
She sits over that wheel every ride.

There's not many left of this model, you know,
The dashboard is genuine wood,
I'd take you a ride round the houses,
But the brakes just don't work as they should.

Are you putting it down in your black book?
Well make sure that your writing is clear,
I'll be reading it back in an hour or two,
I'm the superintendent round here.

ALL THAT GLITTERS

My wife is a picture to look at,
She's a vision of beauty no doubt,
But I wonder if you have the slightest idea
What she looks like before she goes out.

You see when she's at home, she's quite different,
She looks nothing at all like today,
She goes round the house in a headscarf and jeans
And a jumper that's started to fray.

As for manners — you wouldn't believe it!
Nora Batty would beat her on charm,
She'd be far more at home in a coal mine
Or muck spreading down on the farm.

So I think that you've guessed from this insight
Just how much of a job she's to do
Before she sits here looking pretty
And not frightening people like you.

It all starts some three hours before deadline,
She'll say, "I'll just pop up and get changed."
What she means is: the upstairs is right out of bounds
While she gets herself all rearranged.

I don't know what goes off in that bedroom,
She just won't allow me in to watch,
But it takes her two hours to change all her clothes
And pull up her corsets a notch.

Her wardrobe is packed full to bursting,
Every colour and style is in there,
But she starts with her Damart foundation
By deciding what vest she will wear.

When she's dressed she appears in the kitchen
In something alluring and tight,
So she looks fine right up to her neckline
But above that, oh dear, what a fright!

Her make-up is more of a tool kit:
There are lotions and potions and packs,
There are powders and pastes for all different tastes
And some Polyfil just for the cracks.

So then it's "let me have the mirror",
And she takes over that for an hour,
Mind, it all washes off if it comes on to rain
So she won't go out if there's a shower.

Preparing her hair is the last job,
And she pulls it all back to hang down,
And that stretches the wrinkles right out of her face
So there's no way at all she can frown.

When she's put on some scent she's all ready,
And it's then that she blows me a kiss,
And that gives me five minutes to go and get changed
So that's why I turn up like this!

"TAKING IT EASY"

On doctor's advice, 'cause I've not been too well,
I looked round for a restful pursuit,
Something calming and peaceful, away from the strain
Of the work-a-day world of dispute.

At first I thought gliding might be just the thing:
After all, the sky's peaceful and calm,
But then I found out they'd no engine at all
So somehow the appeal lost its charm.

Then a friend said horse riding would help me relax,
Well, riding the horse was all right,
But mucking out stables was part of the job
And I lost all my friends overnight.

Somebody suggested that climbing was fun,
But I found I'd no head for a height,
Last time that I whitewashed the ceiling at home
I looked down and near fainted with fright.

The wife thought I'd like scuba diving:
Swimming free on the ocean sea bed,
But the black rubber suit and the goggles were dear
So I just wore my raincoat instead.

I tried fishing next as a pastime,
"You just sit and relax," I was told,
But after a day sitting on the bankside
The one thing I caught was a cold.

My next venture was clay pigeon shooting,
I joined up with a club for the day,
But I think I need glasses, for all that I got
Was a bull who was three fields away.

Then it dawned on me — take up with gardening:
I've a field right outside my back door,
So I went and bought the equipment,
Though I wasn't sure what it was for.

Well, in springtime I ploughed and I scattered;
In summer I weeded and hoed,
So when autumn came round I thought, "Now is the time
To gather the harvest I've sowed."

Well, the slugs ate up all my potatoes
And the raspberries couldn't be found,
All the flowers were covered in greenfly
But the birds were the fattest around.

By now I was getting quite desperate,
Surely something would fulfil a need?
So I went to the library to get out a book
In order to have a good read.

I thought I'd find something to suit me,
A book that would make me relax,
But what with the cutbacks they'd only one left,
And that was called "Studying Tax".

All these setbacks have really un-nerved me,
I'm so tensed up I could go berserk,
So I'm going to sign off from the doctor's today
And tomorrow I'm off back to work.

"I thought I'd find something to suit me,
A book that would make me relax."

DAFFODILS

Sweet flower of spring, the daffodil,
Tempered by snow and winter's chill,
Gladdening the passer-by
And I.

Softer than summer's garish taste,
Oasis in an earthly waste,
Heralding the warmer days
And haze.

Golden heads mid leaves of green,
Statement of joy unsung, unseen,
Sheltering in wood or gracing lawn,
New born.

Glad daffodil, thou joyous flower,
Proclaiming sunshine mid the shower,
Giving new hope, earth breathes again.
Amen.

STONEGATE, YORK
(A View from Raffles' Upstairs Café.)

What are they saying, those two lovers
                  'neath an umbrella?
She a dufflecoated girl
                  And he a strapping fella.

The jeweller's shop attracts the glance
                  of his young lady fair,
Her finger points the single ring
                  that she would long to wear.

His arm wraps round her in a hug
                  That means "one day, perhaps",
Then, pretending not to care, he motions
                  to the gold watchstraps.

Bending, he gives her hair a kiss
                  And pulls her closer to,
She smiles at him with eyes that say,
                  "Well never mind, you'll do!"

"The jeweller's shop attracts
the glance
of his young lady fair."

FITTED KITCHEN

I rang for a builder last Tuesday
'Cause I wanted a cupboard removed,
So on Friday he came with a spotty young lad
Who was no help at all, as it proved.

The name of the builder was Arkwright,
And this youth who came with him was Jim,
Now I should have smelt trouble the moment he came
For he had all his tools in a tin.

I explained the small job that I wanted,
Which to me sounded simple enough,
But Arkwright looked puzzled, sat down in a chair,
And proceeded to sniff at some snuff.

"Tut, tut, tut," he said after a long pause,
"That will leave a big gap by your door,
And then all your grommets will stick through your posts
Which will make a big hole in your floor.

"You see you've got what's called a low footage,
All the houses this side are the same,
So that means that if I was to leave it alone
You'd get a right smell from your drains.

"What you need is to shift all them cupboards,
Then you see that would give us space,
We could put you a window right under your sink
And you'd get some real light in the place.

"Now while we're on sinks, have you noticed
That your draining board's on the wrong side?
And I can't fit a top at an angle like that
Or the pots that you've washed will all slide.

" 'Now what you want
here is your washer,
I could put it right next to
your drawers.' "

" 'Course you made a mistake with enamel,
Now I'd have got stainless instead,
You see, that will all chip in a twelvemonth,
Whereas stainless would last 'til you're dead.

"Now what you want here is your washer,
I could put it right next to your drawers,
Oh no, I'm forgetting: belay what I've said,
It won't stand the weight on these floors.

"Now see, push that cooker an inch up,
And that would leave room for your hob,
Then plaster straight through with some artex:
Jim's a dab hand at that kind of job.

" 'Course the best thing you've got is your brickwork,
All that wall's made of Cumberland clay,
You'd have twenty more years in that stonework
If your mortar weren't coming away.

"You see, all of your wiring's decrepit,
Your modern stuff's blue, green and brown,
Now Jim knows a good electrician
Who did Safewise before it burnt down.

"Now I know your drive's shared with a neighbour,
So I'll not push this idea too far,
But what about moving that wall out a foot
And ask them to get a small car.

"Do you want me to put it in writing?
See, I'm not one for fancy price tags,
I can tell you right now, 'cause I've written it down:
It's all here on the back of my fags.

"Two thousand should do the job easy,
Well p'raps two and half, but no more,
I can start in the morning at nine, Mr Smith,
You what? Mr Smith lives next door?"

SHORT CHANGED

I can't fathom this decibel money,
It's double dutch if you ask me,
I've just paid 50p in a café:
That's ten shilling for one cup of tea.

It costs ninety pence for a bus ride
And the driver wants that in his tin,
You could go for a bob in old money
And get a conductor thrown in.

Goodness knows what they've done with the coinage,
There's no sixpences left to be found,
And threepenny bits have all gone the same way:
Someone hoarding them all, I'll be bound.

Now there's only five pence in a shilling,
I think Government's trying it on,
There were twelve when we had the old money:
Well where's other seven pence gone?

It's the same with your yards, feet and inches,
You can't go and buy them any more,
They delivered my lino in metres,
Now it's six inches short by the door.

When I was at school we learned tables,
There was rods, poles and perches and yards,
But now if I talk about perches
They think I keep budgerigars.

"There were twelve when we had the old money . . ."

And you can't get a gallon of petrol,
I've tried everywhere, it's no good,
So I have to buy litres to fill up my tank
And the car doesn't run as it should.

I've tried buying two pounds of sausage,
But they've even made that into grammes,
They've mucked them all up and they don't taste the same
So I've gone onto getting boiled hams.

I went for five pounds of potatoes,
But the man said they're kilos today,
So I had to say "five pounds of kilos",
They were only for chips anyway.

I'm fed up with it all, I can tell you,
Now they've started with this "hard ecu"
Well if I find I've got one of them in my change
I shall tell them just what they can do.

A STILL, SMALL VOICE

I have no vision of tomorrow's fate,
No voice cries out to me "This shall be so",
Who shall predict the river in its spate
Or yet return the torrent in full flow?

Age turns and turns the pages one by one,
As from Birth of Time, so this has been,
We live our story, then we too move on,
Interpreting the truth already seen.

Let scholars, preachers, gurus have their say,
Offer redemption, if the gods allow,
Give me a thankful heart to live this day
And be content to know the here and now.

I shall not waste my time in troubled thought
Nor fret unduly when my course is run,
For all my strivings will achieve but naught
And if there be a God, "His will be done".

Good evening, ladies and gentlemen. This evening's poetry reading has been badly affected by a strike of technicians. However, we are being ably assisted by Bert Snoggins, a cleaning operative here at the BBC.

This evening's poem is entitled:

"A CAUTIONARY TALE"

(2nd person.
To be read in flat,
uninterested voice.)

	Soundtrack
The door swung open with a creak	Creak
Then slammed itself again,	Bang
A rat was heard to make a squeak;	Squeak
The roof let in the rain.	Plip plop
High on a shelf, a sleeping cat	Purr purr
Had opened just one eye,	Click
He jumped down from his perch above;	Thud
The rat gave out a cry.	Squeak
The cat's paw caught the lawnmower switch	Click
Which set the mower in motion,	Chug Chug
This ran into a pile of tins	Clang
And made a great commotion	Crash, bang, wallop

34

I made a grab to stop the mower	Grab
But fell over the cat,	Meow
My hand went through a window pane	Crash
And I cried out, "Oh drat."	Oh drat!
Just then, the rat sprang through the hole	Do-ing
Which wasn't large enough,	Ouch
His tail went swishing wildly	Swish
And the cat now called his bluff.	Meow He'h
By now the mower had hit the bench	Bump
Where all the plant pots stood	Rattle rattle
And I raced on behind it,	Tally Ho
But I fell upon some wood.	Oh deary me
My tie got caught up in the blades	Snip snip
Which shredded it in two,	Snip again
It then proceeded up the wall	Chug chug
And took the cat's tail too.	Chug meow
The rat received the same short cut,	Squeak
It's tail fell to the floor,	Plonk
The mower then turned round and crashed	Crash
Out of the garage door.	Crash, bang, wallop
The moral of this story is:	
When you're with friends together,	Chatter
A story can be told again	Chatter
But a tale is gone forever.	Ah!

PARTING

I can't remember if I said "I love you"; I know that's what I intended saying. I had visions of the day weeks before: it would be "Brief Encounter" all over again. You would look small and vulnerable and I would be the quiet hero going away with a stiff upper lip and brave "Goodbye my love, I shall miss you old thing, don't forget to write now and then."

How different things turned out. Losing my ticket like that at the last minute and that station platform packed with holiday-makers coming back from Blackpool and slightly the worse for drink.

I remember feeling hot and cold at the same time and trembling inside with fear and excitement of the future. I was telling myself I would soon be seeing you again, but knowing deep down it could just be a final look at your lovely face. I remember looking long and deep into your eyes, trying to photograph mentally all the little lines and dimples and holding on to your kiss as though my life depended on it.

And then the train rushed in and we both cried silently wiping our tears with embarrassment and making silly conversation about keeping warm and getting a good seat next to a window.

I suppose other people's goodbyes are just as foolish as ours, but now, now we're so far apart, how I wish I could reclaim another minute with you. Hold you again and tell you: you are mine and I am yours forever.

OLD AGE

Day upon endless day,
Weeks and months coming and going
in meaningless monotony.
The net curtains, yellow
now, through age, fall across
the sun and across my thinking.
Just now and then reality
drifts into the whirlpool
of nightmares that are my
companions and I am aware of
my own thoughts.
Why me? Why me, O Lord?
I never thought I'd come to this.

Once I laughed and cried,
Once I loved, oh, how I loved.
I grasped at life's coat-tails
and hung on to the
merry-go-round called "life".
Surely I would stay to the
end, oh yes, others may fall,
but not me, falling off wasn't
me. Why didn't I realise that
everything runs down?
True, I never did fall off,
I just stayed on too long,
'til now I am the only one
left. The everlasting tune
has turned sombre, but plays
on endlessly.
God, how I wish it would end
and let me sleep forever.

DEAD LOSS

My Aunt Edie's just died on her birthday,
In our family she'll leave quite a rift,
If I'd known she was going, I would have held back
And not spent so much on a gift.

She would have been ninety next Tuesday,
We'd booked the Co-op for a meal,
Then her going off in a hurry like that
Was a bit inconsiderate, I feel.

As a girl she loved acting and singing,
She was queen in the music hall days,
She would sing a sad ballad and start to undress
By undoing the lace on her stays.

Of course, she was frowned on by gentry,
She was catcalled and sometimes abused,
She was on the first Royal Variety Show
But Victoria wasn't amused.

They once named a pub after Edie,
Which was quite a strange thing to occur,
They called it "The George and the Dragon",
And there's not much doubt which name was her.

In her lifetime she got through three husbands
Who kept her in diamonds and furs,
Of course, nobody minded the first one,
But the other two husbands weren't hers.

She died of a cold, so they tell me,
It was either a sneeze or a cough,
Mind you, she was mending the roof at the time
And one of them made her fall off.

She was leaving her body to science
But her figure was plumpish and round,
So they told her they'd plenty of dripping
And she wouldn't fetch much to the pound.

On the day she was making her will out
She said, "You'll get a mention, you'll see."
Well the cats' home got all of her money
But she left her best wishes to me.

She wasn't a popular woman,
In fact, I have heard it said
That two of the family both offered a shroud,
And that was before she was dead.

Some say she was tight with her money,
She hung on to her purse to the last,
She would only wear glasses for reading,
Just so that the lenses would last.

Aunt Edie, of course, was a Catholic,
So we had the full service with choir,
The priest waved his handbag about quite a lot,
Then at finish he set it on fire.

He said, "Aunt Edie's not died, she's passed over",
It's a phrase that we Christians prefer,
Then a jumbo jet roared overhead as he spoke,
And I wondered if that could be her.

Uncle Sidney turned up, though he's ninety,
He just looked like a little old gnome,
Then one of the mourners was heard to remark
That it weren't worth his while going home.

She asked that her ashes be scattered
So her soul could have freedom to roam,
But the wind was against me up there on the moors
So I think I've brought most of her home.

Never mind, it's perhaps what she wanted,
For as I tramped back through the ferns
I thought, though she's not here for her birthday
Her ashes are happy returns.

WINTER

Winter's white eiderdown blankets the ground in gentle undulating waves. Tractor wheels zip fasten a seam across a handkerchief field and the sound of its engine falls dead upon the air. A chatter of sparrows squabble momentarily in the hawthorns, powdering themselves in a snow shower. Ice-cream-cornet gateposts drip their over-generous helpings in a plip-plop melody of black puddles. High above in the frosty blueness, a crow circles overhead, searching for a morsel on the white-plate world beneath. Paws of a fox have left a tell-tale pattern beside a dappled wall that comes and goes between snowdrifts. Sheep huddle together in twos and threes, seeking sanctuary from the winter's chill. Only the scarecrow stands erect, maintaining his vigil over the frozen furrows, long since plundered of their bounty. Here and there dark mounds of earth erupt through the smooth whiteness like untidy boils, where the mole has ventured up to sniff the frosty air, only to retreat back into the warmth of his underground home. The frozen dyke lies still now within its shallow grave and the long grasses on either side bow their heads in mourning.

And yet, and yet, within the seclusion of the rill, brave snowdrops offer their tiny florets to the hazy sun, bringing promises of warmer days and a hope of new life.

THEY DON'T KNOW THEY'RE BORN

They don't know they're born, today's youngsters,
It's not like it were in my day,
They come downstairs straight into cornflakes,
We were lucky the days we got hay.

We hadn't no shoes to go out in,
We were known as "Pirellis" in't street
'Cause my dad cut up tyres into pieces
And we had to wear them on us feet.

We didn't know meaning of fashion,
We'd one pair of trousers worn thin,
And my dad always wore them on Sundays,
So rest of us had to stay in.

We were lucky we had got three jackets,
They were cast-offs from't Crimean War,
So me and me sisters were corporals
And my mam was the catering corps.

We'd get up at four in the morning
After sleeping all night on the floor,
Our bedroom was small, so my brother was hung
On a hook on the back of the door.

We'd go off to school wrapped in sackcloth,
And that were a twenty-mile walk,
In our class we all had a slate to ourselves
But we had to share one piece of chalk.

If you fell ill there weren't any doctors,
We'd just get a basin of gruel,
You were happy to lay there half dying
'Cause you wouldn't have to get up for school.

" 'Let's all get round piano,' he'd say,
And many's the night we all stood there . . ."

By the time you were six you went down't pit,
There were one job we all used to dread:
We had to ride ponies and ceilings were low
And by gum, it didn't half hurt your head.

44

When we got home at night we were weary
But Mother would welcome us in,
She'd say, "Sit down to t'table and enjoy your meal,
I've got two ounce of haslet cut thin."

After that, we'd all go on a night shift,
Washing dishes and scraping out pans,
We'd no tap in our house, so it gave us a chance
To wash coal off us faces and hands.

We'd make all us own entertainment,
We'd no toys or games like today
But we used to chuck bricks at each other
To see who could dodge out the way.

My father were't artist among us,
"Let's all get round piano," he'd say,
And many's the night we all stood there
Wishing one of the family could play.

Sometimes I think back to the old days
When I'm signing my name on a cheque,
I think wouldn't it be nice to go back now,
Then I say to myself — "Would it heck!"

WHAT A PERFORMANCE!

Oh my darlings, I wish you'd have seen me
When I was in "Glamourous Nights",
It was just a small part, I was on at the start
As a butler who switched on the lights.

Did I tell you about my King Richard?
My audition was perfect, of course,
I was turned down for King, but I got the next thing:
I was chosen for rear of the horse.

I was in "Carousel" as a barker,
We'd a waterfall built on the set,
But something went wrong as I broke into song
And the first fourteen rows all got wet.

I once played in "Waiting for Godot",
Which wasn't as bad as I'd feared,
It's a two-handed play and I'd nothing to say:
I was God, so I never appeared.

My dears, you'd have loved "Uncle Vanya",
It was all very Russian, you see,
The family are poor and I live next door
And I pop round to borrow some tea.

In "Joan of Ark" I played the jailer,
I remember we toured every town,
But in Crewe I was careless, Joan finished up hairless
And the Tivoli theatre burnt down.

"I went on from that to 'Othello',
When I came on the audience fell dead."

My debut on stage was in Shakespeare:
I performed "A Midsummer Night's Dream",
The papers next day just had one thing to say:
That my "Bottom" had to be seen.

I went on from that to "Othello",
When I came on the audience fell dead,
Of course in those days we'd no make-up for plays
So I did what I could with black lead.

I was very soon up on the West End
In '41 during the war,
I was only a boy, but I loved the Savoy,
And we played in the chapel next door.

I was hailed as a star in "Mikado",
But my costume was really too tight,
When I tore my kimono, the audience cried, "Oh no",
And that show was stopped overnight.

Of course, I've moved on since those heydays,
Drury Lane now is where I will stay,
I'm mobbed every night, and they all push and fight,
But that's just the price I must pay.

Oh loveys, you must come and see me,
I've a dinkie-doo costume that's sweet,
I'll be stood in the porch with a programme and torch
And I'll show you the way to your seat!

A CHILLING STORY

I'm not looking forward to winter,
It comes round the same time every year,
I hate the dark nights and the orange street lights
And the cough on my chest that won't clear.

I'm not one who likes wrapping up well
Every time I step out of the door,
And gloves are no good with my fingers like wood
When I'm fishing for change in a store.

When I wear a flat cap I look silly,
And trilbies aren't me, to be frank,
And a wool balaclava is such a palaver,
I look like I'm robbing a bank.

When it snows some folk go into raptures,
They can't get enough of the stuff,
But I slip and I slide and fall on my backside,
So one day of that is enough.

My long johns are worn out and threadbare,
To fasten them up is a squeeze,
If I try to be slick and put them on quick
My foot goes through the holes in the knees.

And then Christmas comes round every winter
So I have to buy presents and cards,
If I go to a party I have to be hearty
And play silly games like charades.

Some people get kisses at Christmas,
They wear out their lips having fun,
But a pound to a penny I never get any,
I might just as well live with a nun.

I hate queuing for buses on dark nights,
I might stand for an hour in the weather,
I get soaked to the skin and I long to be in,
And then suddenly three come together.

I'm sick of repeats on the telly,
I know "Reach for the Sky" like a rhyme,
You'd think after that scare he'd fly with more care,
But he does the same thing every time.

In the winter the bills are outrageous,
Just to have a hot bath is a pound,
So out of despair I though I might share,
But the woman next door won't come round.

I wish I could be like a dormouse
And sleep all the winter away,
Under blankets and sheet I could dream about heat
And not wake up 'til April or May.

So if you feel like me about winter,
If it gets you despairing and vexed,
When you're frozen and blue and you've nothing to do,
Just remember that spring will come next.

EARLY DOORS

I'm not very good in a morning,
I wake up feeling weary and slow,
My mind says, "It's eight and I mustn't be late,"
But my body says, "Lay still, don't go!"

I once bought myself an alarm clock
To try and make matters improve,
But when it went off, I'd p'raps have a cough,
But the rest of me just wouldn't move.

As a child I was never a riser
I was always the last out of bed,
My mother would shout, "Are you going to get out?
Or shall I have your breakfast instead?"

When the sun shines the rays through the window
And others are starting the day,
All I want to do for the next hour or two
Is sleep all the morning away.

I'm not at my best before dinner,
My features look haggard and long,
The face in the mirror reminds me of Trigger
Or a vest that's been ironed all wrong.

Some people are bright in a morning,
They like to rise up with the sun,
They can get up and go and dash to and fro
While my get up and go has all gone.

I'm clumsy if I'm up too early,
My breakfast just falls in my lap,
And then in my haste, when I squeeze the toothpaste
I get it all over the tap.

My children retreat to a corner,
Well, I don't like them under my feet,
They once said "good morning" without any warning
And what I said I couldn't repeat.

You see, I'm more your afternoon person,
I'm bright as a button at tea,
So if you come round on some matter profound
Ask for somebody else, but not me!

HOSPITAL HOSPITALITY

Oh, you're here, I've been looking all over,
Fancy putting you on the fifth floor!
I'm having a word with that sister
To get you a bed near the door.

And they're no help at all at enquiries,
I've walked round 'til I'm half dead,
I should have come here in the first place
'Cause your grandmother died in that bed.

Well, how do you feel? You look poorly,
Your face is an odd shade of grey,
Your sister went just the same colour as you,
And she only lasted a day.

She would have been sixty this weekend,
It was coming in here killed her off,
The blankets are damp, if you ask me,
'Cause she only came in with a cough.

Some say it were porridge that killed her,
When she ate it she thought it were bad,
And then the nurse came in to bandage her wound
And found it were poultice she'd had.

Well I must say you look a bit peeky,
Have they found out what's wrong with you yet?
I'm inclined to believe Uncle Albert,
After all he's a registered vet.

I was going to bring you some chocolates,
But I thought they might mess up the bed,
And the only shop open was t'chemist,
So I've brought you a toothbrush instead.

These nurses are too young to know much,
And I don't like the language they speak,
If they come round to give you a bed bath
Just tell them you had one last week.

And I'm not very keen on these mixed wards,
You'll be sleepwalking next, I can see,
I've seen how you look at that blonde over there
And you've never looked that way at me.

It's not natural to put men with women,
Your Fred only came in with gout,
They put him in a ward with some ladies
And at finish they carried him out.

By the way are you getting your roughage?
Do things seem all right down below?
Have you told them that some days you're never away
And some days you can't seem to go?

Did I tell you about Mrs Cutthorpe?
You know her with six kids down our road?
Well, her husband's run off with a barmaid:
Her that worked at the "Fishpond and Toad".

"By the way are you getting your roughage?
Do things seem all right down below?"

Just what he saw in her is a mystery,
She's no work of art, I must say,
And her bust is just like shop window
With most of it out on display.

Are you getting the right medication?
These tablets you've got aren't much cop,
They're all different colours, and look at the lid:
This carton says "Smarties" on top.

Goodness me, is it that time already?
I'll have to get back for their teas,
I'm not going to kiss you in public,
So I'll just give your elbow a squeeze.

Now take care, and don't do too much now,
And when you come home, look in pain,
'Cause I've told all the neighbours you've been at death's
*   door,*
I've not mentioned your varicose vein.

ROUGHING IT!

We've decided to take up with camping,
Well, we thought it would make a nice change
'Cause you don't have to do any booking
And you've no digs to pay or arrange.

So we went down to get the equipment
And my goodness, don't things cost a price?
For the money we've paid for the trailer
We could have gone round the world twice.

And the tents come in all shapes and sizes,
Well, we've bought one that's called "Plaza Suite",
Now I'll grant it's a bit on the big side,
But it's fine if we take half the street.

Well, then there was all the equipment
Like the calor gas stove and the hob,
With the pots and the pans, I can tell you
It all came to a tidy few bob.

You see, I was for saving on seating,
I thought deck chairs would just suit us fine,
But the missus insisted we do the job right,
So the table and chairs are in pine.

Now, I told her it wouldn't pack easy,
I said, "Look, it will show every scratch."
She said, "Not if we dine with a tablecloth on
And get carpet and curtains to match."

Now for knives and forks I'd have had plastic,
But my Rita does like some finesse,
So we finished up getting some Sheffield plate,
So the cutlery's EPNS.

Then again, we fell out over lighting:
I suggested a calor gas lamp,
But she's bought this here glass candelabra
That will light up the whole of the camp.

Now most camp sites have modern ablutions,
But for Rita that just wouldn't do,
Well, she's not at her best in a mornings,
So we're taking our own Portaloo.

And of course, she just wouldn't have Lilos,
She said, "You sleep on the floor if you can,
But you're not getting me on an air bed,
I'm having a double divan."

Now I can't get all this in my trailer,
Well, it's too big a job for one man,
So next week when we set off for Cleethorpes
We've got Pickford's to come with a van!

THE ROOM

The bolts were heavy, red with rust,
The hinges gave a wail
As slowly I pushed back the door,
The air was dank and stale.

Within the gloom, a tiny window
Struggled to give light,
But the heavy cobweb curtains
Made the room as dark as night.

I stumbled on a large trunk
That was just inside the door,
Its contents looked like curtains
Half hung out upon the floor.

The shaft of light across the room
Lit up a leather case,
Inside were old newspapers that
Were chewed up into lace.

Suddenly a cupboard door
Swung open to reveal
An army coat and kit bag
And a helmet made of steel.

I groped my way through spiders' webs
To see what else was there,
Then froze in horror as I saw
Two eyes look back and stare.

My heart was just about to stop
With dreadful fear and fright,
Then my eyes became accustomed
To the poorness of the light.

And looking closer at the beast
With staring eyes and scowl,
I discovered to my sanity
A grimacing stuffed owl.

About the floor lay scattered toys
From days of yesteryear,
And wooden barrels that had once
Been filled with flowing beer.

Then suddenly my foot seemed held,
I fell upon the ground,
I laid there in the dust and grime
Afraid to make a sound.

It was then a high-pitched voice rang out
Which froze me to the spot:
"Are you going to clear that garage
Out or not?"

ERNEST
(The Death of a Simple Man)

He was no scholar, no protagonist,
He would not argue matters of great weight,
His face, ill shaven, grimed with dirt,
Seldom could he offer place or date.

Why were we here? Heads reverently bowed
To pay our last respects in sombre mood,
What was this man to we sophisticates?
His intellect naïve, disordered, crude.

His conversation single sentences:
"What time is it?"; "I've got a birthday soon."
His teeth and fingers stained tobacco brown,
A burnt-out pipe would seem his only boon.

We gave him what we could: a timely word,
A helping hand to see the day along,
And in the giving we received the good,
His simple weakness made our weakness strong.

We offer thanks for such a life as his,
We travellers who interwove his span,
For we were privileged to touch his life awhile
And peer at God within this simple man.

BAD CONNECTIONS
(A Husband's Lament)

Hello, this is me, is that you love?
I'm just ringing to see if you're all right,
With it being your first time away love,
That is, to stay more than one night.

Well, how was your journey? All right then?
Did you manage to get a good seat?
You what love? You had to stand up all the way?
Well, in that case love, how are your feet?

Me? Well you know, I'm all right love,
P'raps a little bit tired, that's all,
Only camp beds are not very comfy
And our neighbour's one a bit small.

Well, I had to sleep there for a reason
But I'm hoping to be home tonight,
Once they've shored up the wall in the kitchen
I'm sure things will soon be all right.

Now, don't you go getting excited,
There's no need to shorten your stay,
You stop there and have a good time love
'Cause the gas men are coming today.

No it wasn't my fault it exploded,
Well the firemen said I'm not to blame,
He said, "Chip pans are noted for burning
When they're left for an hour on full flame."

I was only just gone for a minute,
Only next door came round for a chat,
And of course, it all slipped from me mind love
When he said he'd run over our cat.

Anyway, I'm not using the bedroom,
Well it's cold now without any heat,
But the men said they'll put some more slates on
And get rid of the tarpaulin sheet.

Are you seeing the sights with your mother?
She what? She's gone down with the runs?
That's not very good in a wheelchair,
She must weigh a couple of tons.

Oh, I knew I'd some good news to tell you:
You know the new suite that we bought?
Well, I managed to pull it outside love
Before the front living room caught.

Do you like the hotel that you've chosen?
What? They can't seem to fix the lift door?
So you're taking your mother to bed about five
'Cause your bedroom is on the fifth floor?

Well, I don't really know what to say love,
I'd fetch you straight back, you know me,
It's just that the car's out of action
Since I skidded it into a tree.

*"By the way, can you tell me the day you come back?
Hello love? Hello love? Hello?!!"*

Well, you see really that wasn't my fault,
I'd only had one or two drinks,
It was really my secretary's fault love,
Have you met her? They call her Miss Spinks.

No really, she's nothing to look at,
I was taking her home, do you see?
How we both finished up on the back seat
Is really a mystery to me.

You see, she asked me back round to see her place,
She said she'd a spare bed I could try,
Then I don't know what happened precisely
But that's how I got this black eye.

Anyway, that's enough of my troubles,
Has the weather picked up now you're there?
Oh, you haven't stepped out of the hotel
'Cause a wheel has come off your mum's chair.

Still, you'll be glad of the break love,
A change is as good as a rest,
By the way, did I mention the wardrobe was lost
So I've only me pants and me vest?

Oh dear, someone else wants the phone love,
So have a nice time, I must go,
By the way, can you tell me the day you come back?
Hello love? Hello love? Hello?!!

MY COUNTRY

What can I say that has not yet been said
About this blessed land beneath my tread?
This green oasis perfumed by the rain,
Flowing from misty mountain to the plain.

This well-worn tunic patched by farmers' fields
And stitched together where the hedgerow yields
Acre on acre green on every side,
Until at last the land gives way to tide.

Or yet a tiny hamlet comes to view,
Peppered with umber roofs of every hue,
Scattered like confetti mid the trees:
A hodge-podge of man's work formed as to please.

And here a shop falls out into the street
With wares to make the village home complete:
Rugs, tablecloths, tea sets and watering cans,
Prints of old masters, sets of iron pans.

And further on outside the Manor gate
A water pump still stands (not used of late),
Now take the hills and feel the peat beneath,
Or watch the gypsy 'campment on the heath.

Village or farmland, wood or country park,
Mountain or moorland, rich to the eye or stark,
All have a place upon this island strand
That I am privileged to call my native land.

Let those who seek adventure travel far,
Searching to find some other Shangri-la
But I will choose to stay and play my part
Upon this blessed plot that holds my heart.

GREATLY MOVED
(The Saga of Scratched and Mark,
the Two Removal Men)

I'll not tell you again, put your end down,
And don't stub your fags on the floor —
If you must smoke on the Axminster carpet
Put your tab ends out here in this drawer.

By jove, these shepherd's castors are good ones,
I could do with them stuck on my suite,
If she mentions them when we're unloading,
Say they fell off and rolled down the street.

Is it you put your sandwich on this chair?
I've told you about that before!
I've only been sat there a minute,
Now just look at that dralon velour.

And look what you've done with that violin!
It's the last time we'll hear that thing play,
I can just read the name — it's a strada something,
But the other part's broken away.

There's a vase here that she says is priceless
Just because it's marked "Ming" on the stamp,
Well I've seen this same pattern in't British Home Stores:
They're four fifty including the lamp.

"I'm sure you could work a bit faster,
At this rate you'll be here all day."

Stop messing around with them goldfish,
They'll not live out of water like that!
Fancy packing them up like sardines in a tin
And then sticking them next to the cat!

Have you no sense at all with that mirror?
I can tell you've not looked at the plan,
It's the one thing she said she was leaving,
Don't keep bringing it out to the van.

I'm sure you could work a bit faster,
At this rate you'll be here all day,
They'll never believe we were held up by fog:
They've only moved two streets away.

And don't keep on banging that door frame,
That sideboard won't go round the bend.
Go and look in the tool kit, I'm sure we've a saw,
I'll take six inches off of one end.

Well, that's the house emptied completely,
Here's the key, go and give it the man,
You what? He was sat in a green leather chair?
That's the first thing we put on the van!

THE DE GOTNOWTS

We're called the De Gotnowts, we're people of taste,
Of money we've got quite a stack,
Our house is so large we've a car at the front
Just to drive us around to the back.

We mix in high circles with barons and earls,
We have servants at our beck and call,
We've got footmen and waiters and chauffeurs and cooks
And one man for nothing at all.

We only spend twenties and tenners of course,
We throw our loose change on the ground,
We believe in the saying that money's manure:
It's best when it's well spread around.

Some say that we're vulgar, but what do we care?
We could buy then all out in a jot,
They may have a title, but we've got bad taste,
Which is something that they haven't got.

We've a garden that stretches from here to the coast
And could buy acres more if we choose,
Our lake is so vast we've a liner moored up
That we sometimes take out for a cruise.

We often throw parties that go on for days,
After all, we must make a good show,
The deuce of it is that we've not many friends
So we ask people round we don't know.

Our dining room carpet, you wouldn't believe,
Just to lay it it took twenty men,
We once had a corgi who ventured in there
And he's never been heard of again.

When we're ready to dine, we just pick up the phone,
Place our order, then look down the drive,
It's a bit of a chore, but we stand at the door
And wait 'til our pizzas arrive.

We've not worked for years, but open bazaars
And support all the charity do's,
We give them a gift of a tenner or two
And then drink it all back in the booze.

They say that Prince Charlie knows all about us,
But that's not surprising, of course,
For we once knew a girl who went out with a chap
Who had saddled up Diana's horse.

You must make a point, dear, to visit our place,
But do let us know in advance,
We're out quite a lot so we're not often home,
And we must give the royals a chance.

As a matter of fact, I've been thinking all night,
I'd not ask, dear, but oh, what the heck,
We need a lift home, and just one more thing:
Do you think you could cash me a cheque?

WORLD CRUISE

We were watching the telly last Christmas one night
And stuffing ourselves with mince pies,
When all of a sudden this advert came on
And it fair took us both by surprise.

It was offering something quite different, you see
From the usual two weeks in Rhyl,
The pictures were that of a round-the-world cruise
That left never a moment to fill.

Well I looked at the missus and she looked at me
And we both knew what each other thought,
So the very next day we were off down the town
And two round-the-world tickets we bought.

Well we crossed off the days 'til the date came around,
Then we packed all the luggage and that,
We were warned not to take any surplus amounts,
So the wife left her fur coat and hat.

Now we should have been wary when booking this tour,
But we thought that the change would be nice,
You see if we'd have known it was just seven days
We might have thought things over twice.

We'd to meet up at Manchester airport at dawn
And that proved the first of the shocks
'Cause then we were put on an old charabanc
That took us to Liverpool docks.

Our courier's name was Giuseppe Paella,
A nice enough chap in his way,
But the wife said she thought he was foreign because
He was chewing spaghetti all day.

Well we got on this ship called the "Bismarck",
And I thought we'd be in for a rest,
But the captain said, "You've got the room with a view",
And we finished up in the crow's nest.

When we landed in France we transferred to a plane:
A de Haviland something or other,
The wife looked at the pilot and said, "Are you Bader?"
He said, "No I'm not, I'm his brother."

The flight entertainment was well below par,
There was ludo or guessing the mimes,
Then the air hostess warned us to sit to the sides,
'Cause the bomb doors flew open sometimes.

We landed in time to see Venice by night,
There's a city I'll never forget,
But they must have had rain there best part of a week
'Cause just crossing the streets you got wet.

In Spain we ate out on this large balcony
While they danced the flamenco beneath,
But when the wife tried it she'd no castanettes
So she did what she could with her teeth.

Then we sailed through the Suez Canal on a boat
But it's not what it's cracked up to be,
As the wife said, "We've loads of canals back at home,
If that's what we wanted to see."

On Wednesday we went through the Sahara Desert
And prayed that the bus wouldn't stall,
There was mile after mile of this lovely white sand
But nowhere to paddle at all.

When the courier said we'd be visiting Sydney
We all thought of living down under,
But Sidney turned out to be this chap from Leeds,
So that was a bit of a blunder.

In Athens we sailed round the bay in a boat,
And in France we ate frogs' legs and snails,
We saw Venus de Milo, but as the wife says,
"She must have been biting her nails."

In China, of course, we were shown the Great Wall
By this guide who seemed very aloof,
But I said to this chap who was stood next to me:
"You'd think that they'd put on a roof."

We saw so many countries in so many days
I've forgotten just what we saw where,
I remember the wife saying she preferred Greece,
Oh, I wish I'd have left her back there.

As world cruises go, it was really quite nice,
And for two hundred pounds, it's not dear,
But it's not what we'd want to do ever again,
So we'll go somewhere else come next year.

THE COMMITTEE

As chairperson of the committee
May I welcome you all here today,
I can see that we now have a quorum,
So may we please start right away?

Could I first welcome John, our new member?
I've been told that he's just what we need:
A voice of reflection and balance
Which I'm sure we will all want to heed.

Now have we all got an agenda?
Mrs Padlow, perhaps you could share,
I'm afraid you were last to arrive here
And I only put one to a chair.

Could I ask George to read us the minutes
Of the last meeting held here in May?
I can see there were quite a few absent
So you'll be in the dark, I dare say.

Thank you George; now are we in favour?
Could I see that by some show of hands?
Now we come on to "matters arising",
Do you wish to go over the plans?

Could you turn then to page fifty-seven
And paragraph four, section two?
Now you'll see if you look at the small print
That it leaves quite a lot left to do.

Mrs Page, who has now been co-opted
Has formed a committee to see
If, with our constitutional set-up,
We could overlook paragraph three.

You'll remember that back in December
Our treasurer gave his report,
And I seem to recall his misgivings
Over sundry amounts that were bought.

Perhaps Mr Jenkins would sketch out
His proposal of Shrove Tuesday last,
Then I'll call upon Reverend Wilkins
Who will say what was done in the past.

Of course, we could add an appendage,
Mrs Atkins, would you make a note?
Now, if that clarifies the position,
I think we could now take a vote.

I'm sorry to rush the proceedings
But the brownies are wanting the room,
On a show of hands then? Well, that's settled:
The caretaker can have a new broom!

BETTY HILL'S CORNER SHOP

I'm just off to Hill's on the corner
To get something nice for my tea,
I'm not sure what to get, but I've no need to fret,
She's bound to have something for me.

Her shop is a dream for the hungry,
For the sweet tooth, a gourmet's delight,
I've known folk go in looking skinny and thin
And come out with their clothes all too tight.

Her shelves are just sagging with goodies,
She stocks items to fair turn your head,
She sells sweets by the score and she's chocolates galore,
But for more mundane palates, there's bread.

And if you feel poorly or downcast,
She can sell you a potion or pill,
If your doctors despair, she's got medicine there
That will cure you of ailment or ill.

She's got groceries fit for a banquet,
There's tongue or boiled ham by the pound,
She's got peaches and cream and her tarts are a dream,
So you'll need a big bag to get round.

When you look in her fridge your mouth waters,
She's got ice cream to suit every taste,
She's got raspberry jam and some thick marzipan
And yoghurt that just looks like paste.

If you want cigarettes, she's got plenty,
If it's cigars you smoke, she's got those,
But she's only quite small and her shelves are so tall
That she has to stand up on her toes.

Or perhaps you've a child with a birthday,
Well Betty has thought about that,
She's got jigsaws and beads and a dolly that feeds,
Or for babies a cuddly black cat.

Of course, you might just want a paper
Or a magazine for a nice read,
She's got everything there from "Hello" to Voltaire
Or newspapers to suit every need.

And if perhaps someday you're passing
And you think you'll pop in for a chat,
She's a charity bin to put all your change in
So you're sure to got nobbled for that.

She's got something for all of the family,
Your shopping need never be dull,
But a word in your ear just before you go near:
Make sure that your wallet is full.